# A CARTOONIST AND HIS WORK

Of all the tasks required of a cartoonist, coming up with a name or title for a new book is far and away the most difficult and challenging. I thought you might find it interesting thought process-wise if I took you through the steps the Publishers and I went through in determining the title for this collection.

We'll start with the morning I first got the call from the Publishers . . . they were all excited over the idea of doing a collection of my best jokes. They had recently installed a multiple-party conference phone and were anxious to try it out. Within moments the three of us were taking advantage of the new convenience. But before we got into the discussion on the book, Ray, the senior partner, warned me that there might be an interruption, as along with the three-party phone, they had also ordered the call-waiting feature and his partner Mike would be testing it from his Milwaukee office. I could sense this was very important to them and I was in fact glad to be a part of their excitement.

Tom, Ray's assistant, mentioned the problem for the first time. He said, "Joe, . . . there's no sense beating around the bush. We want to do another "Willy 'n Ethel book—a big one—a collection of your best works. And there's no way we can use the same title as the last one. It's just not done. I'm sorry." Ray quickly added, "He's right, Joe."

This really wasn't a big problem for me as all along I'd expected there'd be a different title anyway. As a matter of fact, I was, in a way, kind of surprised the publishers were so concerned about it. But I think it's just their way of being thorough and making sure nothing is taken for granted.

At any rate the situation was now in the open. Mike, the Milwaukee partner, had dropped out of the matter when he learned his title suggestion, "Iacocca" had already been used. So it was more or less up to us to get the job done.

Tom had been compiling research data—statistics, charts and diagrams—that he thought would be useful in helping us target the title's effectiveness. He suggested we meet at their Chicago office to check them over. The most interesting seemed to be the improvement in times for the Decathalon events since 1933. He'd even gone through the trouble of having an artist illustrate some of the events that leaned more towards title suggestions.

Ray, thinking along the same lines, had brought along some photos of his first car that he thought might ring some bells.

We set the material on the table and began to go through it. Tom immediately walked out in a fit of frustration. Ray picked up the photo of his car, he stared at it for a bit, then began turning it at different angles. Finally he folded in two corners of it, and handing it to me said, "See what you think of this."

Tom came back in. Mike was with him. He seemed sheepish and concerned about something. Tom pushed him in front of me saying, "Go ahead, tell him . . . Tell him what you did." What had happened, as it turned out, was that they hadn't actually gotten the call-waiting service. Mike had been outside on an extension phone that he had plugged into their line. There was a little commotion. I could see Ray was more embarrassed and hurt than anything. But eventually we settled down to work on the title.

For a few hours we batted around the idea of which page the title should go on. Ray, thinking everyone puts it on the cover, suggested why not in the middle for a change.

There were several phone calls and each time Mike reached for it claiming he had the call-forwarding service and had arranged for them to come to this number. Tom laughed out loud for a while. Ray just looked down at the floor, shaking his head. Mike, trying to get the subject off him and back to the book title, suggested we call it "Area Code Willy 'n Ethel" and have a fold-out center page like Playboy. Only instead of a nude girl have all the nation's area codes in the shape of a giant phone.

Tom thought about it for a minute and then asked Mike if he could see his wallet. When Mike gave it to him, he took the scissors and began cutting the contents into tiny strips. This took some time and when he finished he put it all in a little paper bag. You could see by the look on Mike's face that this wasn't the first time this kind of thing had happened to him.

Ray took a "back-to-business" tone. The problem, technically stated, seemed to be getting a title that would, as quickly as possible, get the idea across to the public that this was a collection of the best jokes of Willy 'n Ethel as opposed to, let's say, a gun catalogue or a side of beef.

Mike was measuring the phone cord when Tom stood up, pointed to me, and said, "Rave on . . . The Buddy Holly Story."

And were it not for a last minute suggestion, that's what it would've been.


## The End

AL'S
HOME OF THE WORLD'S
GREATEST STEW
CHILI
SOUP
TEA
CATSUP
WATER
CARD TRICKS
SPFTTT

"OH, NO!"

"WE'RE OUTA RYE, HOW ABOUT WHOLE WHEAT ?!"

"WILLY.. I WAS THINKING..LAST NIGHT WE HAD A BIG ARGUMENT... WELL, SOMETIMES WHEN PEOPLE HAVE ARGUMENTS THEY SAY THINGS THEY DON'T MEAN.. I JUST WANTED YOU TO KNOW I NEVER DO THAT "

"YOU'D BE SURPRISED HOW MANY OF THESE I GO THROUGH EACH WEEK "

"I CAN'T TELL YOU ENOUGH WHAT A KICK MY BRIDGE CLUB GETS OUT OF YOU TWO "

"WILLY...THE GIRLS AND I WERE TALKING AND YOU'RE NOT GOING TO BELIEVE WHAT WE'VE FIGURED OUT IS THE REALLY SICKENINGEST THING ABOUT YOU "

"BE HONEST, ETHEL, THE TRUTH IS IT GRIPS YOU WITH TERROR
TO SEE ME TAMPERING IN THE MYSTIC ARTS "

"LET'S SAVE SOME FOR TOMORROW...IF THERE'S ONE THING I
LIKE BETTER THAN PIZZA, IT'S BREAKFAST IN BED "

"YA KNOW, THIS PROVES HOW GOOFY YOU ARE!...YOU COULD'VE GOT ME THE BEER, FOUND THE T.V. PAGE AND CHANGED
THE CHANNEL IN ONE-TENTH THE TIME IT TOOK TO PACK ALL MY THINGS!"

"THERE ... A HALF-GALLON OF MILK, A LOAF OF BREAD, TWO LAMPSHADES AND A GOLF BALL ... WHO SAYS I NEED A LIST!"

"HOLD IT, MAC, WHERE I COME FROM THE ONE WHO PAYS GETS TO SHOOT THE CORK"

"DO I LIKE MY JOB!? I'D BETTER LIKE IT!! IT COST ME 80 THOUSAND DOLLARS' WORTH OF PLASTIC SURGERY"

"TELL ME THIS... CAN YOU REMEMBER ANY TIME IN YOUR LIFE WHEN YOU MAY HAVE UPSET ANY GYPSIES?"

"I HATE TO RAIN ON YOUR PARADE, FRIEND, BUT THAT TIME WASN'T FOR KEEPSIES"

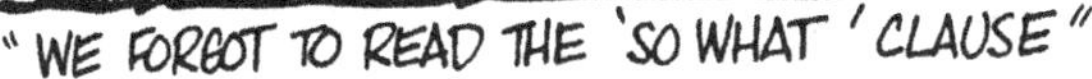

"WE FORGOT TO READ THE 'SO WHAT' CLAUSE"

"SHE'LL BE BACK... SHE'D NEVER LEAVE WITHOUT HER FAVORITE RAG"

"AND FIND OUT IF THEY'RE LOOKING FOR SOMEONE WHO'S SELF-MOTIVATED...
I DON'T WANNA BE MAKIN' A TRIP DOWN THERE FOR NOTHING!"

"UNDERNEATH ALL THESE LAYERS OF SCREAMIN' YELLIN' UGLY FAT THERE'S A
QUIET, SHY, SKINNY GUY WHO NEVER SAYS NOTHIN'... THIS PIECE IS FOR HIM"

"MYRON HAS THE WORLD'S LARGEST COLLECTION OF STYROFOAM SHAPES AND NO ONE'S THE LEAST BIT SURPRISED"

"HERE WE ARE WASTING VALUABLE TIME TRYING TO FIND SOLUTIONS WHEN WE SHOULD BE ARGUING OVER WHO'S TO BLAME!"

"GERONIMO"?!?
JOE MARTIN
12-1

YOUR HUSBAND'S SUGGESTION TO AIR YOUR PROBLEMS THROUGH A PROGRAM OF STRUCTURED COUNSELING AND FAMILY COOPERATION CERTAINLY SEEMS PRACTICAL...

ON THE OTHER HAND, IT'S HARD TO FIND FAULT WITH THIS PLAN OF YOURS TO SKIP TOWN ON THE NEXT BUS
6-13
JOE MARTIN

WOOPS!
CLONK
CRONCH
HERE...WE'LL JUST PUT ALL THE PIECES BACK IN THE BOX, THEN PUT IT BACK ON THE PEDESTAL AND SHE'LL NEVER NOTICE
2-10

JOE MARTIN
7/16
"THE MORE I LOOK AT THIS PICTURE OF YOUR SISTER YAWNING WITH HER MOUTH WIDE OPEN, THE MORE I BEGIN TO REALIZE JUST HOW INFINITESIMAL THE UNIVERSE REALLY IS"

"THEY'RE DROPPING LIKE FLIES...EASE UP ON THE FOOD COLORING"

"WHAT SCARES ME THE MOST IS THE SURPRISED LOOK ON YOUR FACE"

GOOD NEWS AND BAD NEWS, UNCLE WILLY... FIRST THE GOOD NEWS...
YOU CAN STOP LOOKING FOR THAT GAS STATION
4-17
JOE MARTIN

"SO...YOU DON'T KNOW WHY YOU'RE 'ALWAYS TIRED' EH?!... I'LL SHOW YOU 'ALWAYS TIRED'!! I'LL SHOW YOU 'ALWAYS TIRED' !!! WIPE THAT LOOK OFF YOUR FACE! "

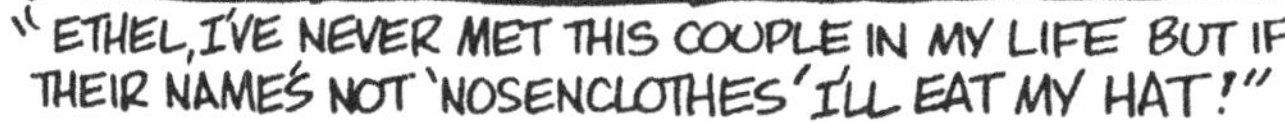
"ETHEL, I'VE NEVER MET THIS COUPLE IN MY LIFE BUT IF THEIR NAMES NOT 'NOSENCLOTHES' I'LL EAT MY HAT!"

"WHADDYA GOT THERE, HON, ONE OF THEM BRAIN TEASERS ?"

"SEEMS LIKE ONLY YESTERDAY I WAS ASKING YOU TO GET OUT OF BED"

"MY FERNWELL'S GOT A MEAN STREAK THIS LONG"

LOAN YOU MONEY ?! ABSOLUTELY !! HERE..
TAKE AS MUCH AS YOU WANT !!

ETHEL.. THE CATERER IS HERE

"`TWO OVER EASY`, HE SAYS... IF ONLY THEY KNEW..
EH, LEON ?!"

"YOU'LL BE TALKING TO `ALL OF IT NOW` JOHNSON "

"ALL RIGHT, I'LL APOLOGIZE TO YOUR SISTER AND TO SHOW YOU HOW SINCERE I AM I'LL DO IT IN THE VOICE OF DONALD DUCK, HER FAVORITE CARTOON CHARACTER "

"I HOPE YOU DON'T THINK I'M USING THIS AS AN EXCUSE, BECAUSE WE REALLY WOULD LIKE TO HIRE YOU, BUT IT'S JUST TOO WINDY "

"WELL, ETHEL, LOOKS LIKE I GET THE LAST LAUGH.. THEY TURNED DOWN YOUR APPLICATION TO HAVE ME REGISTERED AS A NATIONAL LANDMARK"

"LET ME PUT IT THIS WAY, MURPH ... IT'S A MAYBE, BUT IT'S NOT A STRONG MAYBE"

"DON'T TELL ME, LET ME GUESS.. YOU'RE SELF-CONSCIOUS ABOUT YOUR HEIGHT?. YOUR HAIR?. YOUR WEIGHT?.. YOUR NOSE?. AM I GETTING WARM?!"

"THE TRICK TO A MUSTARD, CATSUP AND RELISH SANDWICH IS PLENTY OF RELISH"

"WELL THEN, HOW MUCH WOULD THE HALF SLICE OF BREAD BE WITHOUT THE GRAVY?"

"...SET YOUR INJECTION MOLDING MACHINE AT..."

"OKAY, HON, KEEP THAT SPRAY ON...I'M GONNA TRY AND TURN THOSE BURGERS"

"THAT'S NICE, YOU WENT BACK AND GOT A TIE...BUT I'M AFRAID NOW YOU NEED **TWO** TIES!"

"FRANKLY, WILLY, I DON'T THINK ANYONE THINKS WE'VE GOT AIR CONDITIONING".

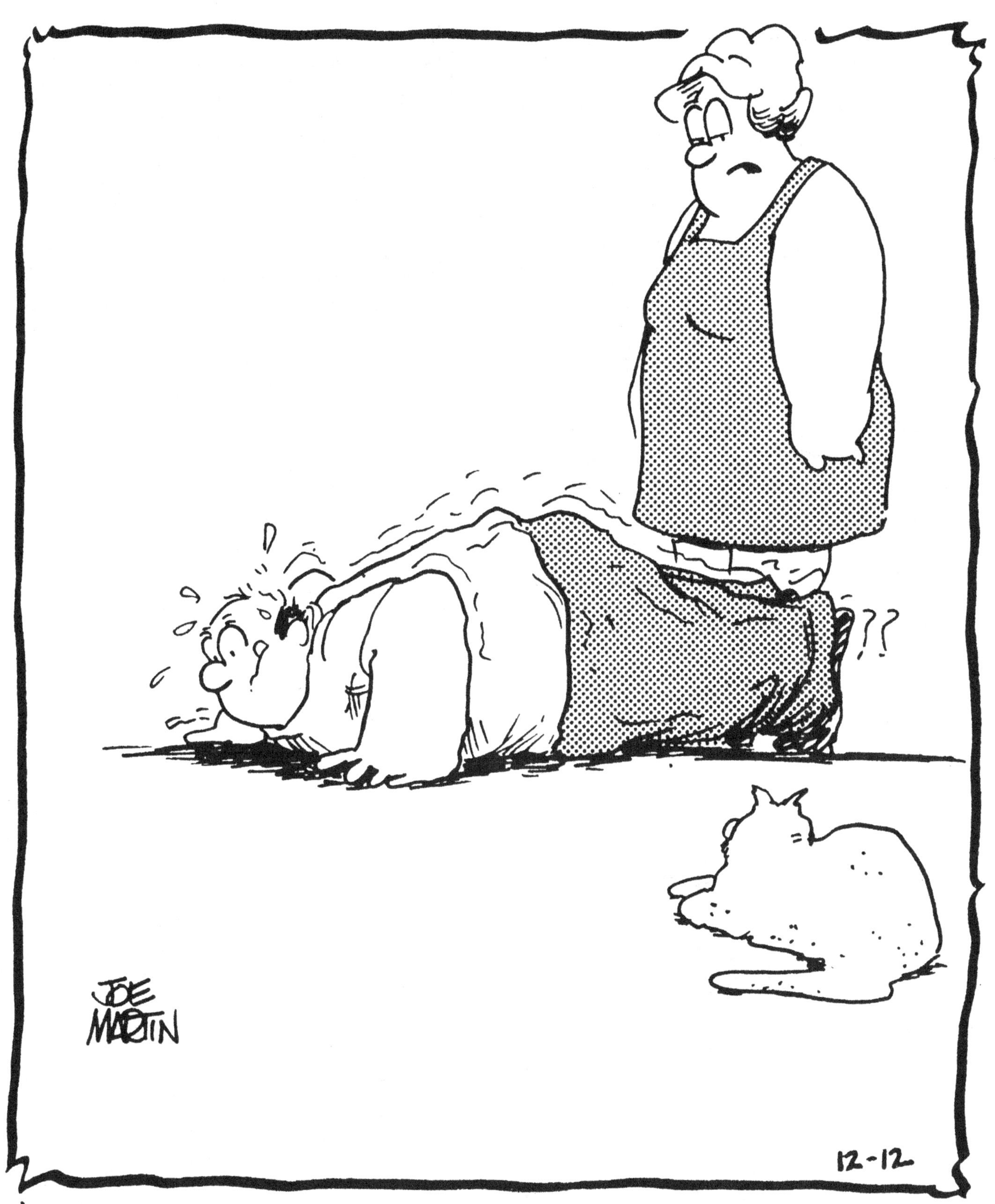



"ONE ONE-THOUSANDTH OF A PUSH-UP... TWO ONE-THOUSANDTHS OF A PUSH-UP..."

"THERE WASN'T ANY BREAD SO I HAD TO MAKE IT INTO A BALL ... YOU WANT HALF?"

"I'LL HAVE WHAT THE GUY ON THE END'S HAVIN'!"

DOC!! I GOTTA TELL MY WIFE THAT SOMETHING'S WRONG WITH ME!!..
IF I DON'T SHE'LL HAVE ME PAINTING THE WHOLE APARTMENT!! YOU GOTTA HELP ME, DOC!. YOU GOTTA GIMME SOMETHING TO TELL HER!
2-3
HON... BAD NEWS... ONE OF MY OARS IS OUT OF THE WATER
JOE MARTIN

EMPLOYMENT
HELP WANTED
JOE MARTIN
4-19
"C'MON, TELL ME....WHY DID YOU REALLY COME HERE?!"

9-16
JOE MARTIN


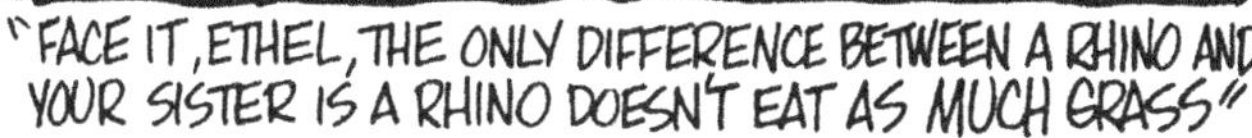

"FACE IT, ETHEL, THE ONLY DIFFERENCE BETWEEN A RHINO AND YOUR SISTER IS A RHINO DOESN'T EAT AS MUCH GRASS"

CAT, FETCH MY SLIPPERS!
HEY, DO YOU HEAR ME?!
FETCH MY SLIPPERS!
BIF
PLOOP
3/12
I HOPE THIS AIN'T THE LAST OF THE MILK 'CAUSE IF IT IS I'M IN BIG TROUBLE!
JOE MARTIN

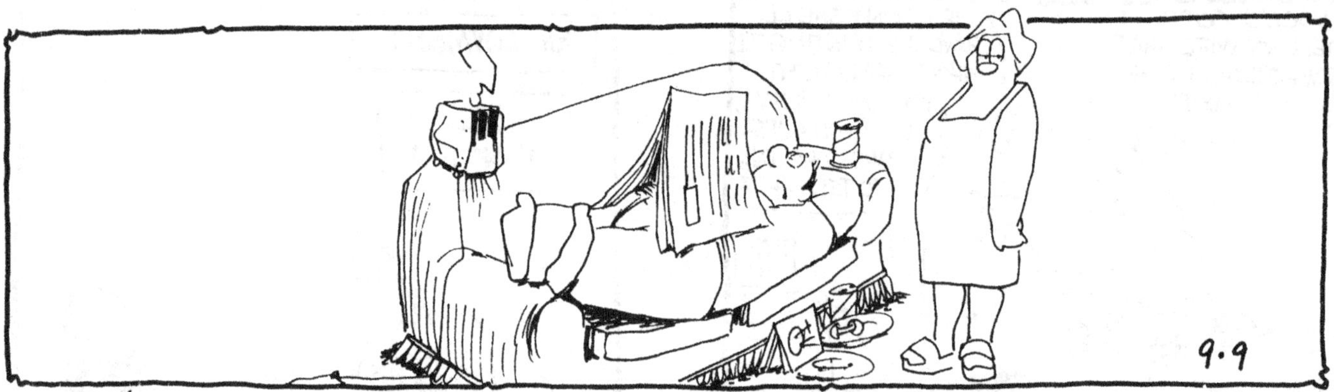


"IT'S TIME PEOPLE REALIZED LAZINESS IS A DISEASE, AND SHOULD BE TREATED LIKE ONE!.. IT'S NO DIFFERENT IN ANY WAY FROM GOOFING AROUND OR DAYDREAMING!"

"SO, IT'S ANOTHER TAILGATER, IS IT?!! RIDING RIGHT ON MY BUMPER!! WELL, WILLY, YOU KNOW HOW I HANDLE THESE CLOWNS!!"

"DO YOU REALLY THINK HE BELIEVES IT'S FOR THE CAT?"

"I DON'T CARE WHAT THE FINANCIAL COUNSELOR SAYS, I'M IN THE MOOD FOR A CLASSIC CASE OF MISHANDLING FAMILY FUNDS"

"HOW MANY TIMES HAVE I TOLD YOU, YOU'RE SUPPOSED TO WAIT TILL THEY TURN AROUND"

"TOO BAD!.. A MOMENT SOONER AND WE COULD HAVE PROCESSED YOUR APPLICATION IMMEDIATELY"

"JUST THINK OF US AS YOUR FRIENDS... THE LOCUSTS"

" WELL, WELL, DON'T WE LOOK SPIFFY !.. WHAT'S THE OCCASION ? "

"ALL RIGHT...HOW MUCH DO YOU NEED TO GET THE T.V. FIXED ? "

" REMEMBER WHEN I CAME TO PICK YOU UP FOR THE SENIOR PROM AND YOUR SISTER MADE THAT REMARK ABOUT MY SUIT RIGHT IN FRONT OF EVERYONE AND I JUST STOOD THERE LIKE A DUMMY WITH MY MOUTH HANGIN OPEN....YA KNOW WHAT I SHOULDA SAID!?"

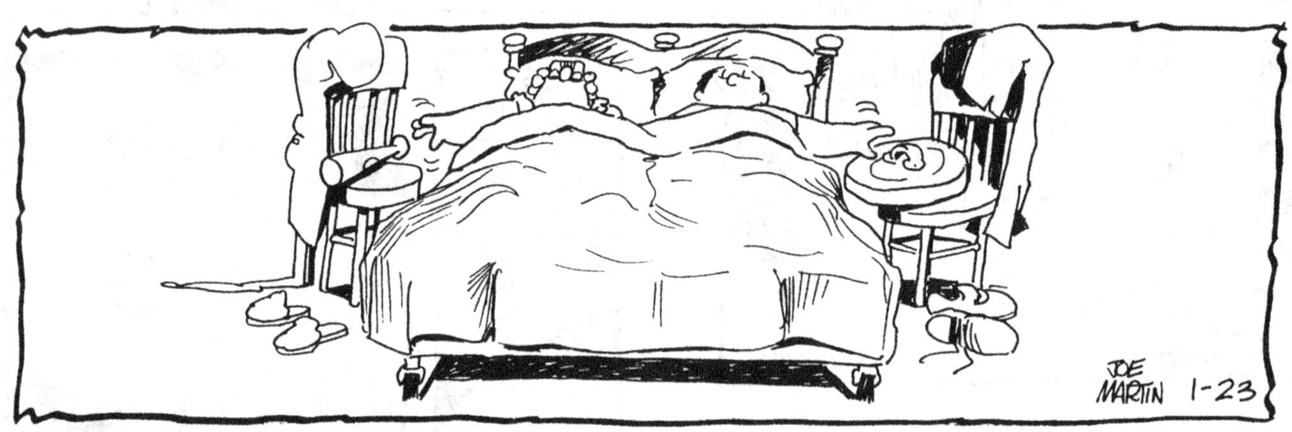

"WORLD'S LARGEST LIVING MAMMAL AND I
DON'T EVEN GET A GLIMPSE ... THAT'S THE
LAST TIME I SIT BEHIND YOUR SISTER"

"THEY PROBABLY THINK WE'RE A PAIR OF
FANTASTICALLY RICH MISERS "

"WAIT ONE SECOND WHILE I FINISH THIS LETTER...
BEFORE YOU'RE OFFICIALLY LAID OFF I'D LIKE
YOU TO LICK THIS ENVELOPE "

" I GOT THE REFUND BUT DON'T DAWDLE..
I TOLD 'EM YOU HAD A GUN "

" I THINK I SEEN THIS ONE AT THE SHOW, THE SPECIAL EFFECTS
ARE FANTASTIC!..HE NEVER DOES CATCH THE MOUSE, THOUGH...
I THINK HE GETS SUCKED INTO A VACUUM CLEANER "

"HERE'S SOMETHING YOU'LL LIKE..VERY CHIC AND ALLURING...,
IT'S THE LATEST THING, WE CALL THEM `BAGGY DRAWERS´"

"OK, LET'S SPEED THINGS UP AND SET A TWENTY-MINUTE LIMIT ON THE SHAKING OF THE DICE "

"GO AHEAD AND LAUGH.. BUT I HAD IT APPRAISED AND THEY SAID IT WOULD BE WORTH 20 THOUSAND DOLLARS IF IT WASN'T PLASTIC "

"OKAY, WILLY...YOU'RE NEXT"

"CALL ME PSYCHIC, BUT I'LL BET THAT'S OUR NEPHEW"

"IT WAS MUCH BETTER THE LAST TIME WE WERE HERE... OF COURSE THEN WE WERE CLOSER TO THE FRONT WHERE IT'S NOT SO PICKED OVER "

"HIS NAMES SNAKE, BUT THEY CALL HIM RON "

"LOOK! THIS ISN'T 'BLOOPERS AND PRACTICAL JOKES'...NOW STOP ASKING!! "

"I'M SORRY BUT I'M AFRAID YOUR LOAN WAS TURNED DOWN BY ONE OF THE GIRLS IN THE TYPING POOL"

"FIND THE GUY THAT PUT UP THIS SIGN!. I WANT HIM TO HEAR THIS!!"

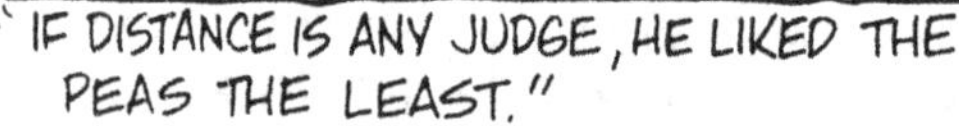

"IF DISTANCE IS ANY JUDGE, HE LIKED THE PEAS THE LEAST."

"I'M AFRAID IT'S CROSSED THAT THIN LINE THAT SEPARATES THE FINE RUNNING MID-SIZED CAR FROM A GIANT RADIO"

"GO AHEAD, WILLY, SHOW THEM THE ADDITION YOU PUT ON"

"START FRESH, BUILD A NEW LIFE ... YOU'LL GET OVER IT"

"HEY!...TURN YOUR HEAD WHEN YOU SNEEZE!"

"WELL, MISTER 'KINGPIN OF CRIME', WHAT DO I DO WITH A BASEMENT FULL OF HUBCAPS?"

I'M GONNA HAVE TO GIVE YOU A PRESCRIPTION
COULDN'T WE HANDLE THIS SOME OTHER WAY?

TOO LATE NOW, PAL, I'VE ALREADY STARTED WRITING IT
5-3
JOE MARTIN

JOE MARTIN
6-6
COME TO BED, WILLY..YOU'RE ONLY TORTURING YOURSELF..NOTHING ANYONE
SAYS OR DOES IS GOING TO BRING THAT PIECE OF CAKE BACK "

9-30
JOE MARTIN
"WELL, THEN, I GUESS IT'S ALL GONNA COME DOWN TO
WHO CAN STAY AWAKE THE LONGEST "

I READ THE GOVERNMENT PAYS 400 DOLLARS FOR WASHERS JUST LIKE THAT
FOUR HUNDRED DOLLARS!
ETHEL, WE'RE RICH!
JOE MARTIN
3-28

"OK, GENIUS, IT'S MY MOTHER, THINK FAST! WHY AM I LIVING IN A BASEMENT WITH A FAT DWARF?"

"I THINK THEY GOT THE HINT... HE SAID THEY'D LEAVE WHEN THEY FELT LIKE IT"

"HOW LONG WOULD IT TAKE YOU TO MAKE 120 MILLION OF THOSE ?! "

"HON..YA WANNA COME OUT FROM UNDER THE BED FOR A MINUTE?..THAT GOOFY BOLTS COME LOOSE AGAIN!"

"ALL RIGHT, I THINK WE'VE PUT UP WITH ABOUT ENOUGH OF THIS!"

ETHEL, WHAT WOULD YOU SAY IS MY MOST OUTSTANDING TRAIT?
WILLY, YOU DON'T HAVE ONE OUTSTANDING TRAIT
1·21
YES.. GO ON

"WATCH IT.. LOOK OUT... YAAAA !?? ETHEL, THIS HAS TO BE ONE OF THE WORST HOROSCOPES I'VE EVER HAD ! "
8·8

"AND HERE'S OUR SPECIAL ANNIVERSARY PATTERN... IT COMES IN MINUTES, WEEKS, MONTHS OR YEARS "
JOE MARTIN
9·10

ETHEL, I WANT YOU TO KNOW THAT NO MATTER WHAT HAPPENS I'LL ALWAYS BE BY YOUR SIDE
DON'T THREATEN ME, BUSTER
1·14

" NOW TRY IT "

" THEY DID A NICE STORY ABOUT YOUR LITTLE TRAFFIC INCIDENT... PICTURES AND ALL ...
THEY EVEN MENTIONED YOUR NAME...THE ONLY CLOUD I CAN SEE IS THEY MISSPELLED 'MANIAC' "

"IT'S A SPECIAL AWARD, THEY GIVE IT ONLY ONCE EVERY DECADE...I'D RATHER NOT TALK ABOUT IT"

"THAT'S THE SPOT WHERE HE STANDS WHEN HE RAKES THE LEAVES"

"WHADDYA THINK... TOO PRACTICAL?"

"YOUR SISTER ASKED US OVER FOR DINNER...I TOLD HER WE COULDN'T MAKE IT...BUT DON'T WORRY, I SMOOTHED IT OVER...I TOLD HER WE HAD A BULB GOING OUT"

"GET UP, WILLY... YOU'LL BE LATE FOR WHATEVER IT IS YOU DO"

" ' THE EARTH SHOOK, THE SKY RUMBLED, AND A VOICE SAID," NOAH, IF YOU MISUNDERSTAND ME ONE MORE TIME I'M GOING TO MAKE IT RAIN FOR 40 DAYS AND 40 NIGHTS...NOW GO OUT AND GATHER TWO OF EVERY ANIMAL IN THE WORLD AND BUILD FOR THEM A GIANT PARK. " ' "

" STILL NO WORD FROM MOTOWN ? "

"TELL ME THIS, AND BE HONEST, IF YOU HAD YOUR LIFE TO
LIVE OVER, WOULD YOU WATCH ANYTHING DIFFERENT ?"

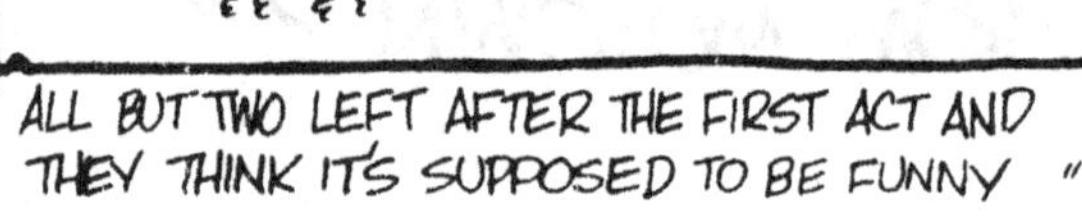



"ALL BUT TWO LEFT AFTER THE FIRST ACT AND THEY THINK IT'S SUPPOSED TO BE FUNNY"

"NO, REALLY! FRANCINE IS A FANTASTIC VENTRILOQUIST... I JUST MOUTH THE WORDS..THAT'S WHY WE GET ALONG SO WELL ...DIDN'T YOU EVER NOTICE HOW SHE NEVER DRINKS WHEN I'M TALKING?"

"OK, LET'S GET SERIOUS AND SKIP THE FIDDLING AROUND... FIRST ONE TO GET HIS HORSE ACROSS WINS "

"SHE'S SLEEPING SO PEACEFULLY I ALMOST HATE TO WAKE HER"

"GOOD NEWS!...THEY MADE IT LEGAL NOW TO BUY THAT SUIT YOU WANTED"

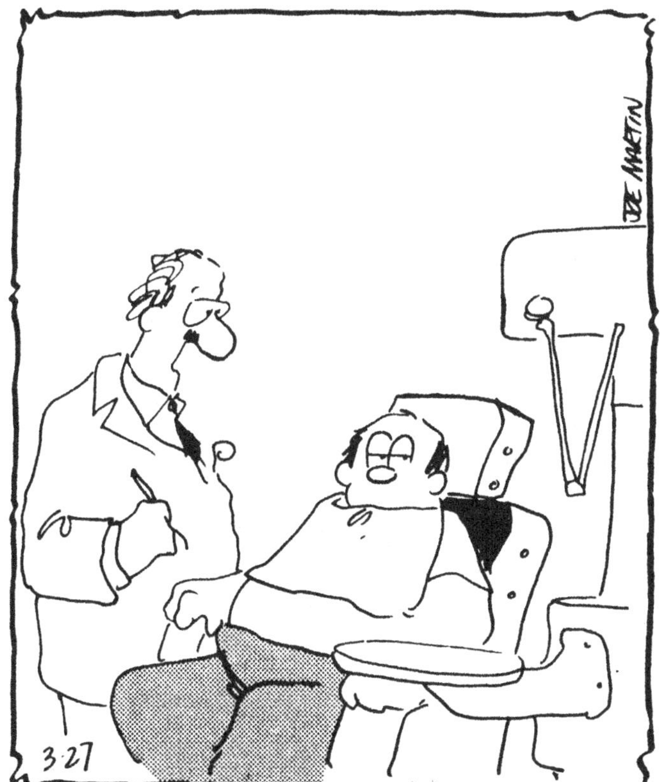


"I'LL BE HONEST WITH YOU...ONCE THE NERVE'S DEAD I JUST SEEM TO LOSE INTEREST"

" SO THIS NICKNAME ` MISTER LUCKY'... IT REALLY
DOESN'T MEAN ANYTHING "

OK, HON.. WHADDYA WANNA DO TONIGHT? STAY
HOME AND WATCH T.V... GO TO THE TAVERN AND
WATCH T.V.. OR GO TO YOUR
SISTER'S AND WATCH T.V. ?
WHY DON'T WE
HAVE A NICE QUIET
DINNER AT THAT
QUAINT LITTLE
CAFE BY THE
WATERFRONT?
WHEN DID THEY
GET A T.V. ?

A GIANT AMONG DWARFS,
A DWARF AMONG TURTLES,
A TURTLE AMONG ROACHES,
AND A ROACH AMONG ANTS
NEVER MIND...
I'LL WRITE MY
OWN INTRODUCTION

NOW THERE'S
TWO OF
US THAT CAN
MAKE A
TREE
HOW ARE
YOU ON
SCREWBALLS ?

"WHEN THE WATER REACHES THIS LEVEL THE WALLS AUTOMATICALLY BEGIN TO CLOSE IN... WHEN IT'S FULL THE SQUID CHUTE OPENS. IT'S THE FLASH GORDON ROOM AND FRANKLY IT'S NOT ONE OF OUR BIG SELLERS"

"IT'S GOT THAT 'LIVED-IN-BY-MANIACS' LOOK"

"OH, HON.. HERE'S A CUTE ONE"

"ETHEL, IF THESE FIGURES ARE ACCURATE THAT LAST PARTY HAS JUST ROCKETED COUCH CUSHIONS INTO THE NUMBER ONE POSITION AS OUR LEADING SOURCE OF INCOME"

" LET'S TURN IT ON... ANYTHING'S BETTER THAN THIS "

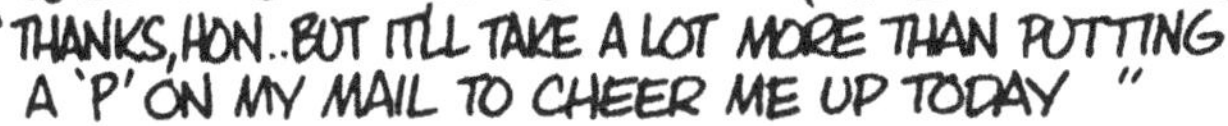

"THANKS, HON.. BUT IT'LL TAKE A LOT MORE THAN PUTTING A 'P' ON MY MAIL TO CHEER ME UP TODAY "

"IN HOLLYWOOD THEY SAY YOU'RE ONLY AS GOOD AS YOUR LAST PICTURE...I REALLY HATE TO END THE DAY WITH THIS CLINKER"

"AND HERE'S OUR GAME ROOM... WOULD YOU CARE TO PLAY THE WORLD CHAMPION?"

"WHEN MORT AND LEON SING 'TO ALL THE GIRLS I'VE LOVED BEFORE' THERE'S NOT A DRY AIR-SICK BAG IN THE HOUSE"

"TOO BAD THESE AREN'T BEER TREES"

"IF WHAT HE SAYS IS RIGHT HE'S DOOMED TO SPEND THE REST OF HIS LIFE IN THAT BED....THERE'S NO KNOWN CURE FOR A FORCE FIELD"

"I'M SURE I PAID THAT BILL!! I DISTINCTLY REMEMBER PUTTING THE CHECK IN THE BOTTLE!..YOU KNOW WHAT MUST'VE HAPPENED?!..I'LL BET THAT CRAZY CORK POPPED OUT!"

"HERE COMES ANOTHER ONE THAT CAN'T READ"

"WHAT ARE THEY UPTIGHT ABOUT?! DIDN'T YOU TELL THEM I MIGHT ALREADY BE A WINNER?"

"IT LOOKED SO LONELY"

"THAT'S NOT AN AUTOMATIC CHANNEL CHANGER INTERCEPTOR, IS IT?"

"YA KNOW, HON, WE'VE REALLY GOT A LOT TO BE THANKFUL FOR... BEANWISE, THAT IS!"

"NOW I DON'T WANT YOU TO THINK I'M BEING SMART-ALECKY.. BUT YA KNOW WHAT WOULD REALLY GO GOOD WITH THIS ?!! ..... PAINT!"

"THE BAD NEWS IS WE'RE TURNING YOUR LOAN DOWN!.. THE GOOD NEWS IS IT'S THIS KIND OF DECISION THAT HAS KEPT US NUMBER ONE IN OUR FIELD!"

"YA KNOW, YOU'RE RIGHT... THIS ISN'T AS EASY AS IT LOOKS "

IF I SELL 'EM ALL IT'LL WORK OUT TO SOMEWHERE IN THE VICINITY OF 180 BILLION DOLLARS AN HOUR
$85,000.00
$120,000

LOOK, A WILLY PENCIL!...SHORT, STUBBY, NOT VERY SHARP AND THERE'S REALLY NO POINT TO IT
4-21

"BARGAIN KING" BOUGHT THREE ROOMS OF FURNITURE FOR UNDER A HUNDRED DOLLARS
JOE MARTIN
9-23

"CAPITALIZE 'CREDIT MANAGER,' PUT A COMMA BETWEEN 'ADDITIONAL LIABILITIES' AND 'FINANCIAL PRESSURE,' A PERIOD AFTER 'REALIGN INSTALLMENT SCHEDULE' AND HYPHENATE 'PIG-FACE.'"

"HE ALWAYS STARTS SHOWIN' OFF WHEN HE GETS THE LEAD"

"NOT COUNTING HUNGER, WHAT WOULD YOU SAY IS THE STRONGEST HUMAN EMOTION?"

"WELL, HON, I FINALLY GOT MOST OF THAT PAINT SCRAPED OFF ONE SIDE OF THAT LIGHT SWITCH...BY THIS TIME TOMORROW I SHOULD HAVE A DARN GOOD START ON THE REST OF IT"

"THE GUY THEY HIRED TO REPLACE ME STILL HASN'T SHOWN UP AND ALREADY THEY'VE NOTICED A MARKED IMPROVEMENT"

"WOW!. VANITY PLATES!! GEE, HON, THANKS!!"

"YA KNOW WHAT WOULD REALLY HIT THE SPOT NOW?.. A COCONUT!!"

8-26
"OK, FINE... DO IT YOUR WAY... BUT DON'T COME CRYING TO ME
WHEN IT DOESN'T COME OUT WITH A PEARL-LUSTRE FINISH!"

OK, WILLY, FINISH
THIS SENTENCE...
BEHIND EVERY GREAT
MAN THERE'S A...
I KNOW IT'S EITHER
A COUCH, A CHAIR OR A PILLOW
BUT I'M NOT SURE WHICH
JOE MARTIN 2-24

"IF ALL YOUR PAYCHECKS FOR THE LAST 5 YEARS WERE LAID END TO END THEY'D FORM A MAGNIFICENT HIGHWAY STRETCHING ALMOST TO THE DOOR"

"AND IF IT'S TOO DEEP, YOU SIMPLY PUSH DOWN ON THE WATER-LEVEL CONTROL VALVE CONVENIENTLY ATTACHED TO YOUR ANKLE"

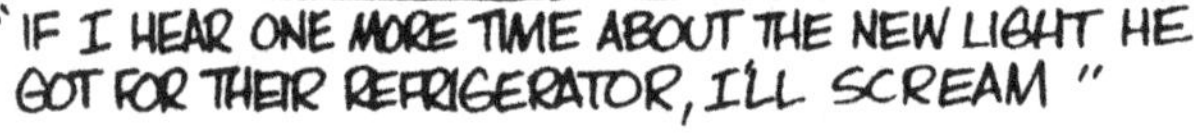
"IF I HEAR ONE MORE TIME ABOUT THE NEW LIGHT HE GOT FOR THEIR REFRIGERATOR, I'LL SCREAM "

" OH, GREAT!...THIS IS YESTERDAY'S PAPER ! "

"I'LL BE HONEST WITH YOU, MORT, I DON'T EVEN LIKE THIS STUFF "

" ARE YOU THINKING OF A LOVED ONE ? "

"MY HANDS ARE OCCUPIED WRITING THIS DOWN, BUT, PLEASE.. TRY TO IMAGINE MY INDEX FINGER EXTENDED, POINTED TOWARDS MY EAR AND ROTATING AROUND IT "

"THEY'RE GETTING THE HIGH-PRESSURE HOSE OUT... LOOKS LIKE ANOTHER 'NO' "

"T.V. REPAIR?... THAT'S PAGE 1672, HON"

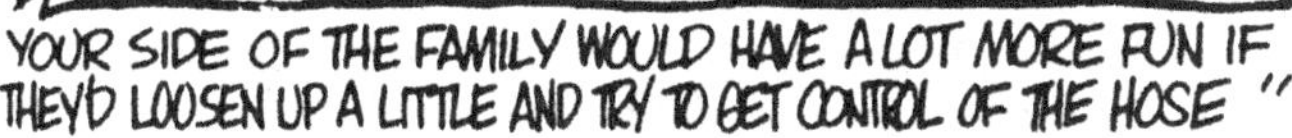

"YOUR SIDE OF THE FAMILY WOULD HAVE A LOT MORE FUN IF THEY'D LOOSEN UP A LITTLE AND TRY TO GET CONTROL OF THE HOSE"

HEY, ARE YOU BY ANY CHANCE RELATED TO SMELSO 'THE FATS' BALDOREENIO ?! "

THERE'S TWO KINDS OF BEER IN THE REFRIGERATOR
WHAT'S THE MATTER, HON... LIFE GETTING TOO COMPLICATED?

SOME BEARS ARE KNOWN TO HIBERNATE FOR LONG PERIODS, RARELY MOVING... TOTALLY IMMOBILE FOR SOMETIMES AS LONG AS SIX MONTHS

TURN SOMETHING ELSE ON, THIS IS HITTING TOO CLOSE TO HOME

ETHEL.. I'VE PUT OFF FIXING THIS TOASTER LONG ENOUGH... THROW IT OUT ! "

NOW REMEMBER .. MY SISTER IS VERY SELF-CONSCIOUS ABOUT HER NOSE
OH, THAT'S CUTE !.. THEN, WHERE AM I SUPPOSE TO HANG MY COAT !?
7-1
JOE MARTIN


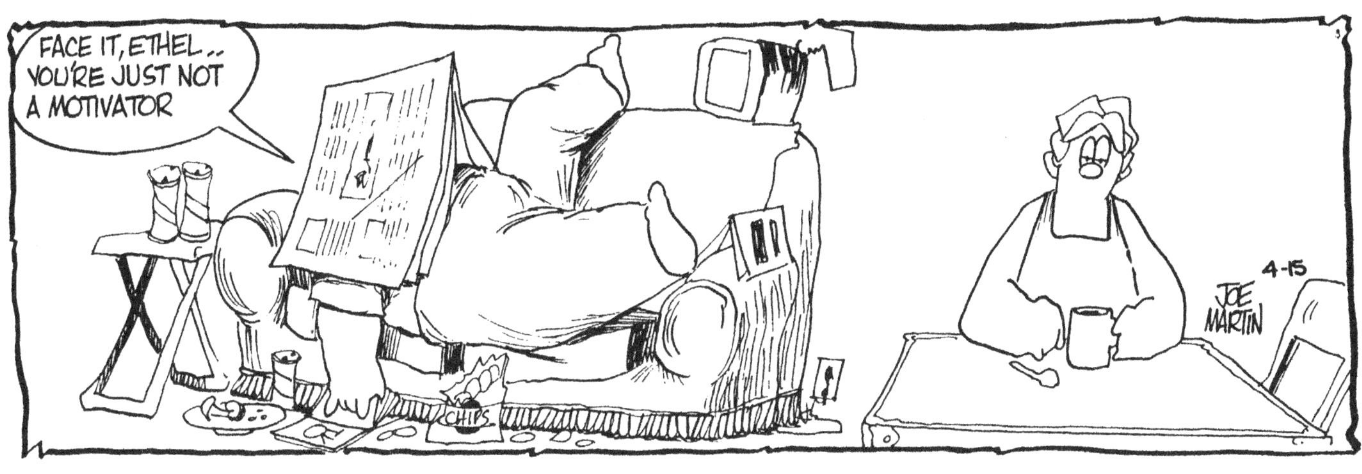

FACE IT, ETHEL .. YOU'RE JUST NOT A MOTIVATOR
CHIPS
JOE MARTIN
4-15

WHAT'S THE FLASHING LIGHT?
IT'S THE LATEST THING .. THEY CALL 'EM FUZZ BUSTERS ..
IT LET'S YOU KNOW WHEN YOU'RE GONNA GET A TICKET

"THERE NOW, THIS SHOULD FIT"

"THEY'RE KNOWN HERE FOR THEIR LITTLE CRACKERS WRAPPED IN CELLOPHANE"

"I'M SORRY... MISTER WEAVER CAN'T SEE ANYONE RIGHT NOW... HE'S TAKING OVER FOR HIS SECRETARY!"

"EVER WONDER IF THERE'S PEOPLE ON OTHER PLANETS THAT'LL LOAN US MONEY?"

" OH, BREAK DOWN... DON'T BE SO CHEAP "

" IF I HAD ANY GUTS I'D APPROVE THIS LOAN OF YOURS AND JOIN THE CIRCUS "

EACH DAY MORE AND MORE FISH BEGAN DISAPPEARING....
BUT I DIDN'T PUT TWO AND TWO TOGETHER UNTIL THE CAT EXPLODED

THEY LET ME DRINK OUT OF A GLASS GLASS TODAY!..THEY ACTUALLY TRUSTED ME WITH A GLASS GLASS!. THEY BELIEVED IN ME...THEY HAD FAITH IN ME!..
BUT I LET THEM DOWN... I LET THEM DOWN BADLY!
YOU HAD TO BE THERE TO APPRECIATE IT
4-29

DO YOU THINK THEY'LL EVER COME UP WITH A WAY WHERE WE'LL BE ABLE TO WATCH ALL THE T.V. PROGRAMS AT THE SAME TIME?
I HAVE A FEELING IT'S ALL GOING TO BE UP TO YOU
JOE MARTIN   2·17

"DON'T FORGET TO KEEP YOUR EYES CLOSED UNTIL YOU KNOW WHICH WAY ITS POINTED "

"BUT, WILLY, IF YOU FIT IN, IT WOULDN'T BE A GRAND SCHEME "

"HE'S LISTED THE MACHINES HE CAN OPERATE IN ORDER OF PROFICIENCY... NUMBER ONE IS THE AUTOMATIC COIN CHANGER "

"I SAW THE LIST OF PEOPLE TO BE LAID OFF.. MY NAME WAS THE ONLY ONE SURROUNDED BY A RAINBOW, STARS AND UNDERLINED IN RED... WHAT DO YOU THINK IT MEANS?"

WHILE YOU WERE IN THE SHOWER YOUR SISTER MADE A REAL GAME EFFORT AT STOPPING BY

OK, WE'RE GONNA DO THIS JUST LIKE A RESTAURANT...
WOULD YOU LIKE BREAKFAST NUMBER ONE, BREAKFAST NUMBER TWO, OR BREAKFAST NUMBER THREE?
WHAT'S BREAKFAST NUMBER ONE?
COFFEE WITH CREAM

SOMETIMES ON A CHEAP CUT OF MEAT YOU'LL FIND A PIECE OF GRISTLE... WOULD YOU RATHER HAVE THAT THAN ME?

WHAT GIRL WOULDN'T?

I CAN HANDLE DRAGONS, FIRE-BREATHING MONSTERS, STRANGE VISITORS FROM OTHER PLANETS, EVEN TROLLS... BUT NORMAL EVERYDAY PROBLEMS SEEM TO GET ME DOWN

" THE DIAL BUSTED OFF.. HE YELLED, ` I CAN'T CONTROL IT'... THEN HE FAINTED "

"SURE IT MAY BE A TRICK, BUT THEN AGAIN IT MAY NOT BE... THE QUESTION IS.. CAN YOU AFFORD TO TAKE THE CHANCE?"

"TO ANSWER YOUR QUESTION I NEED FIRST TO KNOW THE NAME OF THE JOCKEY"

"ARE WE THERE YET?"

"HE USED TO THINK THE WHOLE WORLD WAS AGAINST HIM, BUT NOW HE'S NARROWED IT DOWN TO ONE GUY WITH A HOSE"

"COME TO BED, DEAR, YOU'VE DONE ALL YOU CAN.. I'M SURE THE PIECE WILL TURN UP SOMEWHERE "

"GOSH, FLOYD, IS THERE ANYTHING YOU CAN'T DO!?"

" YOUR SISTER CAN SIT WHEREVER SHE WANTS, BUT IF SHE'S WEARING HER WIG I HIGHLY RECOMMEND HERE ! "

"HOLD ON!"

"I'M SORRY.. I DON'T KNOW THE VOLUME RULES OF ETIQUETTE ON REMOVING OLIVE PITS"

"BELIEVE ME, ETHEL, WHEN I FINALLY COME TO THE POINT YOU'LL UNDERSTAND WHY IT WAS IMPORTANT THAT I BEAT AROUND THE BUSH"

"LET ME PUT THIS IN TERMS YOU'LL UNDERSTAND.. UNLESS YOUR NEPHEW LEARNS HIS MATH HE'LL NEVER BE ABLE TO HANDICAP HORSES"

LOOK AT THIS!...IF THEY CAN PSYCHOLOGICALLY CONDITION SOMEONE TO WALK ON HOT BURNING COALS WHY CAN'T THEY PSYCHOLOGICALLY CONDITION SOMEONE TO GO OUT AND GET A JOB!?
C'MON, HON, BE REALISTIC.. WHICH WOULD YOU RATHER DO?
4·28

MY GRANDFATHER HAS THE FIRST DOLLAR HE EVER MADE FRAMED AND HANGING ON HIS WALL
SOMEDAY SO WILL YOUR UNCLE WILLY
SOON, HON... DON'T FORGET TO SAY "SOON"
JOE MARTIN
CHIPS

WELL, THAT'S IT FOR THE EVENING NEWS.. AND WE COULDN'T HAVE ENDED WITH A MORE BIZARRE STORY...THANK YOU AND GOOD NIGHT!
NOW...WOULD YOU LIKE TO HEAR MY SIDE?
10-30
JOE MARTIN

"BAD NEWS, WILLY, THERE'S ONLY SIX LEFT, SNEEZY'S GONE"

"ON THE PLUS SIDE IT'S ECONOMICALLY IMPOSSIBLE FOR US TO HAVE A MAJOR SETBACK"

"I'LL HAVE A COLD PIECE OF CHICKEN, A HALF A BANANA AND WHATEVER'S LEFT IN THAT CARTON OF MILK"

"TIMES ARE CHANGING BUT UNTIL THE PUBLIC FULLY ACCEPTS CARRYING HANDGUNS I REALLY DON'T SEE YOU AS AN EFFECTIVE SALESMAN"

"YOU'RE IN LUCK.. THE DOCTOR'S IN A VERY GOOD MOOD TODAY... AGAINST ALL ODDS HE WON A VERY IMPORTANT MALPRACTICE SUIT ON AN OBSCURE TECHNICALITY "

"FLOYD'S BEEN WORKING ON YOUR CAR FOR TWO DAYS AND SO FAR THE ONLY THING HE CAN FIND WRONG IS THE HOOD WON'T OPEN "

"THEY'RE HOME ALL RIGHT, THEY'RE JUST NOT ANSWERING THE DOOR "

"I WENT TO STIR THAT STUFF YOU HAD COOKING ON THE STOVE AND THE SPOON BROKE OFF... IF THAT MEANS IT'S DONE, YOU MADE WAY TOO MUCH!"

YOU'RE NEVER GONNA GET A JOB...
YOU'RE JUST GONNA LIE THERE AND
DO NOTHING... SLEEP! SLEEP!
SLEEP!. THAT'S ALL YOU'RE
EVER GONNA DO !!
3·11
JOE MARTIN
DON'T STOP

"LOOK, FEENEY THE MAILMAN'S BEEN UP AND ON THE JOB FOR OVER SIX HOURS AND YOU HAVEN'T EVEN FINISHED PUTTING MUSTACHES AND BEARDS ON THE MORNING PAPER"

"IT'S ONE OF THEM TRICK MIRRORS..THEY USE 'EM TO STEER THE CUSTOMERS TOWARDS THE HIGHER-PRICED STUFF"

"LIFT THAT GATE, BOY, IT'S TOLL GATE TOMMY...
HE RIDES FREE!"

"I'LL BE HONEST WITH YOU..I'M NOT REAL GOOD AT THIS, PIG EYES"

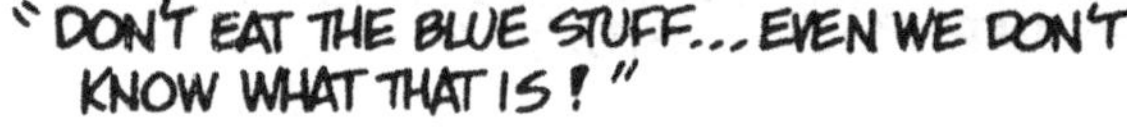
"DON'T EAT THE BLUE STUFF... EVEN WE DON'T KNOW WHAT THAT IS!"

UNCLE WILLY... HOW LONG WOULD IT TAKE YOU TO RUN A HUNDRED YARDS?
THAT'S HARD TO SAY... I'M FORTY-FOUR AND I STILL HAVEN'T

THE LOGICAL THING TO DO IS CUT OUT BOWLING, MOVIES, DRINKING AND EATING OUT UNTIL OUR BILLS ARE PAID
HEY
NOW!
BILLS
ETHEL, I ONLY WISH I HAD A TAPE RECORDER SO YOU COULD HEAR HOW RIDICULOUS WHAT YOU JUST SAID SOUNDS
BILLS

HA.. YOU SHOULD'VE THOUGHT ABOUT THAT BEFORE YOU MARRIED HIM...
CHIPS

"'WAS WILLY HERE?' SHE SAYS... NO, LADY.. IT WAS
OMAR THE ORIENTAL STEEL BENDER.. GIMME A BREAK!"

"MUST BE THAT GOOFY MURPHY...WHO ELSE WOULD RING FOUR HUNDRED TIMES ?!"

" WAKE UP, BABE... SIGN'S ON! "

"WELL, HERE IT IS, HON, THE FINAL FIGURE... DO YOU WANT IT IN DOLLARS AND CENTS OR WHAT IT ACTUALLY MEANS IN BEER?!"

"ETHEL, WHAT I HAVE TO TELL YOU MIGHT COME AS A SHOCK..IT MIGHT BE BETTER IF YOU SAT DOWN AND LET ME TIE YOU UP FIRST"

"20 DOLLARS TO LEARN HOW TO THROW YOUR VOICE IS A LOT OF MONEY TO SPEND JUST SO YOUR FRIENDS WILL THINK YOUR CAR'S GOT A TALKING COMPUTER "

" SHE ASKED ME IF I'D LIKE A T.V. DINNER... WITHOUT THINKING I SAID, 'SURE, WHY NOT?' "

YOU'VE GOT THE T.V. ON, THE RADIO BLARING, YOU'RE READING A COMIC BOOK AND YOU'VE GOT MAGAZINES ALL OVER THE PLACE!
YOU'RE RIGHT, HON... I'VE GOT TOO MANY IRONS IN THE FIRE
JOE MARTIN

I WANNA SHOW YOU SOMETHING. THIS IS ONE OF ETHEL'S DONUTS
DUNK DUNK DUNK
SQUISH
SPLOT
NOW WATCH
5-5
IN A MINUTE IT'LL POP RIGHT BACK TO ITS ORIGINAL SHAPE
JOE MARTIN

HOW MANY TIMES DOES A PERCOLATOR PERK TO MAKE A POT OF COFFEE?
REGULAR OR ELECTRIC
UNEMPLOYMENT TRIVIA
3-31
JOE MARTIN

"THEY BOTH KNOW IT'S NOT A MIRROR BUT THEY'RE JUST TOO STUBBORN TO ADMIT IT"

"HI, HON, I'M HOME... AND FOR ONCE I'D APPRECIATE IT IF YOU'D SKIP THE 'WHOOP-DE-DO'"

"I JUST HAD AN EERIE THOUGHT... WHAT IF NEITHER ONE OF US IS KEEPING SCORE?!"

" MAYBE YOU'RE NOT EATING ENOUGH RAW FISH "

"NO COMMERCIAL BREAKS FOR THE REST OF THE PROGRAM!! WHAT KIND OF THING IS THAT TO SPRING ON A GUY AT THE LAST MINUTE?!!"

"I'LL COME BACK LATER WHEN YOU'RE NOT SO BUSY"

"YOU CAN HAVE YOURS FREE.. WE NEED SOMEONE TO START THE BALL ROLLING "

" THIS SOUNDS GOOD.. IT'S ABOUT A SPACE MONSTER WHO'S FALLEN INTO A TIME WARP DURING A DIMENSIONAL FREEZE WITH PROBLEMS JUST LIKE YOU AND ME"

"ONLY A LUNATIC WOULD WEAR SOMETHING LIKE THIS ! "

"DON'T HIT THAT SNACK TRAY TOO HEAVY...I WAS JUST KIDDING WHEN I SAID WE WERE INVITED"

"VEER, YOU IDIOT, VEER !!"

"WE'RE GONNA TAKE A TEN-MINUTE BREAK NOW"

"I THINK, IF YOU TWO WILL TAKE A CLOSE LOOK AT THIS CHART I'VE PREPARED, YOU WILL GET A CLEARER IDEA OF JUST HOW MUCH YOU ANNOY ME"

"YOUR UNCLE WILLY'S TELEPATHICALLY SIGNALING FOR A BEER.. BRING HIM THIS BEFORE HE HAS A STROKE"

"TOO BAD WE'RE NOT OUTSIDE...THOSE FLIES ON THE CEILING WOULD BE STARS "

" YOU SHOULDA BEEN THERE, HON, WHEN MURPHY FINISHED SINGING '99 BOTTLES OF BEER ON THE WALL' THERE WASN'T A DRY EYE IN THE HOUSE "

HOW COME YOU'VE GOT THE T.V. SO LOUD?
ASK YOUR GOOF-NUT SISTER, SHE'S THE ONE OUT THERE LEANIN' ON THE DOORBELL
JOE MARTIN

AUNT ETHEL...IS CABOOGLIO A WORD?
ONLY IN SCRABBLE AND ONLY IF YOU'RE PLAYING YOU KNOW WHO
JOE MARTIN

HOW HIGH DO YOU THINK YOU'D HAVE TO SCORE ON THAT TO GET INTO HARVARD?
BIP BIP BIP
GEE, HON, I DUNNO..BUT I IMAGINE IT WOULD REALLY HAVE TO BE SOMETHING...THAT'S A PRETTY GOOD SCHOOL
PCOOCH TIC TIC TIC TIC
JOE MARTIN

"THIS IS THE PART WHERE HE BECOMES KING OF THE ACCOUNTANTS AND TAKES OVER ALL THE BOOKS"

"BE A GOOD BOY AND THE NEXT TIME YOUR UNCLE WILLY DOZES OFF I'LL LET YOU POUR SOME OF THIS ON HIM"

"NO WE DON'T GIVE VOLUME DISCOUNTS FOR OVERDRAFTS.. BUT I AM GLAD YOU ASKED "

" CAREFUL WHAT YOU SAY.. HE'S THE ONLY ONE WHO KNOWS WHERE THE DOOR IS "

"NO, REALLY, WE MUST GO... ARE YOU SURE YOU CAN HEAR US IN THERE !? "

"C'MON, WILLY... GIVE IT UP....LET'S GO.. YOU'RE NEVER GOING TO CATCH THE OTHER ONE "

"WHADDYA THINK?.. THEY'RE ETHEL'S IDEA... SHE SEWS 'EM ON ALL MY CLOTHES... THEY'RE LITTLE WEASELS"

"ETHEL, I'M NOT IMPRESSED WITH ANY OF YOUR TITLE SUGGESTIONS FOR MY EXERCISE BOOK!.. LEAST OF ALL 'FATSO GOES TO BALLOONVILLE'"

"FACE IT, ETHEL, IF IT WASN'T FOR THOSE FEW GIANT CARD FORTS MY LIFE WOULD BE A TOTAL WASTE"

"THE BAD NEWS IS THAT'S A FIFTY-THOUSAND-DOLLAR VASE AND THERE'S NO WAY TO GET IT OFF WITHOUT BREAKING IT... THE GOOD NEWS IS YOU'LL NEVER HAVE TO SHAVE AGAIN"

I JUST HAD A TERRIBLE THOUGHT...
WHAT IF THE WAY YOU WEAR YOUR HAT HAS NOTHING TO DO WITH HOW MUCH MONEY YOU MAKE ?!
JOE MARTIN

SUPER FUDG-O BARS 27¢ EA.
WHEN I WAS A KID THEY WERE A QUARTER

CROSS YOUR FINGERS... ONE MORE DUD AND IT'S BACK TO THE NUT FARM
JOE MARTIN

"ALL RIGHT..WHAT IS IT ?! I CAN TELL BY THE ANGLE OF
THE TOASTER THAT YOU'RE IN ONE OF YOUR MOODS AGAIN"

"THEY'RE REALLY PROUD OF THEIR JOBS..ALL THEY
TALKED ABOUT WAS WHAT TIME THEY HAD TO GET UP"

"I'M GLAD I'M A GIRL...I COULDN'T HANDLE BEING BALD AGAIN"

"FIDDLE WITH THE BUTTON A LITTLE...MAYBE IT'S JUST OUT OF FOCUS"

"IT'S HARD TO BELIEVE THAT THESE ARE BETTER FOR YOU THAN CIGARETTES"

"RELAX.. WE'VE GOT PLENTY OF TIME ... THEY'RE NOT EVEN TAPPING THEIR FEET YET"

"AHA!.. SHE'S MADE A FATAL MISTAKE!.. THE ADVANTAGE IS OURS... SHE'S LOST THE ELEMENT OF SURPRISE"

"FLOYD'S HOBBIES ARE GENETIC ENGINEERING AND FOOD... GET READY TO DUCK"

"HE'S WAITING FOR HIS BIG BREAK ...3 COMMERCIALS IN A ROW"

"ETHEL...WOULD YOU PLEASE TAKE THAT TOAST OUT OF YOUR HAIR?! YOU HAVE NO IDEA HOW FOOLISH IT MAKES YOU LOOK "

"WOULD YOU LIKE ME TO PULL THE SHADES?... I CAN DO THAT FOR THE KIND OF MONEY YOU'RE TALKING"

"THE GOOD NEWS IS THEY'LL SETTLE FOR EIGHT DOLLARS... THE BAD NEWS IS THEY WANT IT ALL AT ONE TIME"

WILLY TALKS IN HIS SLEEP BUT IT'S SO BORING IT'S RESTFUL"

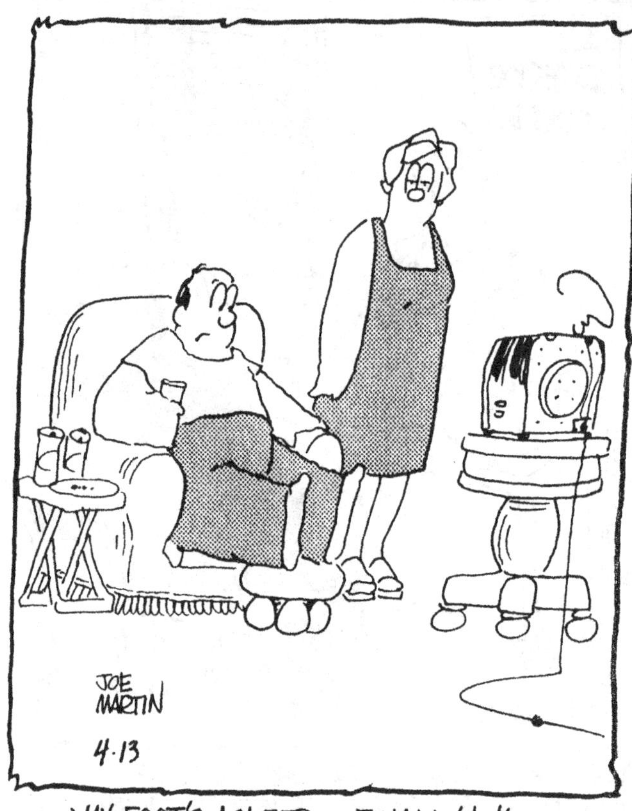


"MY FOOT'S ASLEEP... FINALLY!"

"WE'RE NOT OUT TO IMPRESS ANYONE, THE PLAIN ONE WILL DO"

"HERE.. I THINK IT'S THE SIGNAL YOU'VE BEEN WAITING FOR.. THEY WANT YOU TO GO TO THE STORE AND GET A HALF GALLON OF MILK AND A LOAF OF BREAD"

"NOT COUNTING 'SHAKE WELL', WHADDYA THINK IS THE MOST COMMON INGREDIENT FOUND IN MOST MEDICINES?"

UH, OH.. THE ARROW...
THIS NEARLY ALWAYS
MEANS TROUBLE
OUT
JOE MARTIN

"ACCORDING TO THIS ARTICLE EACH ROOM SHOULD MAKE A STATEMENT...
THIS ONE'S MUST BE `KABOOM !' "

" HOW COME WE'RE SO STUPID?! THAT SOUNDS LIKE ONE FOR JOLTIN' JOHNNY... HEY, J. J. ! "

" WHADDYA MEAN HE CHANGED HIS MIND ?!! WE ALREADY WENT !! "

"THIS GUY SAYS THAT LOUSY LAUNDRY DETERGENT I FOUND
IN THE ALLEY HAS A STREET VALUE OF 80 MILLION DOLLARS..
YOU CAN TELL HE'S NEVER USED IT"

HEY, ETHEL...IF YOU HAD YOUR CHOICE WHAT WOULD YOU PICK?.. BEING ABLE TO SPEAK FIVE LANGUAGES FLUENTLY...
OR ONE REAL GOOD!

CLOSEOUT SALE
CASH AND CARRY
ALL SALES FINAL
NO REFUNDS NO EXCHANGES
"AND THE GREAT THING IS IF YOU DON'T LIKE IT..
THAT'S TOUGH!!"

WILLY, YOUR FAVORITE SHOW'S ON... "MISTER DULL"
"IN TONIGHT'S EPISODE MISTER DULL FINDS OUT THE TIME FROM AN UNEXPECTED SOURCE!"
HMMM!... SOUNDS LIKE A TWO-PARTER!

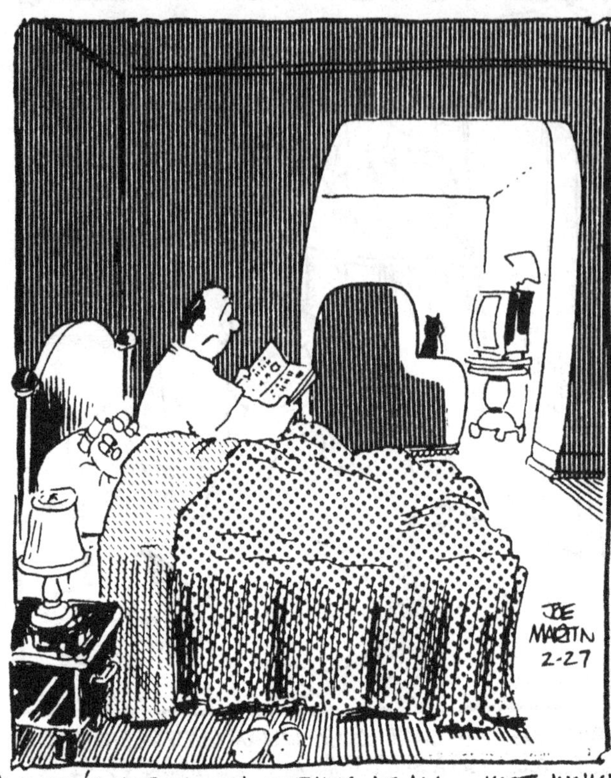


" THERE'S NOTHING ON.. NOTHING AT ALL ... JUST JUNK!
THAT CAT'S NUTS !! "

"I REDID THE ENTIRE KITCHEN...THE CHAIR IS WILLY'S TOUCH"

"OK, WE'LL PUT IT TO A VOTE...WHAT WOULD YOU RATHER DO?..FLOAT AIMLESSLY FOR DAYS OR GO REAL FAST FOR A FEW SECONDS?"

"I SEE YOUR AUTOMATIC CHANNEL CHANGER'S ON THE BLINK AGAIN"

"I DIDN'T SAY ANYTHING AT THE PARTY... BUT THAT COMMENT YOU MADE ABOUT ME 'SURROUNDING YOU WITH OPULENCE'... HOW DID YOU MEAN THAT?"

"OK, NOW, WATCH CLOSE.. IF EVELYN WOOD COULD INTERVIEW, THIS IS HOW SHE'D DO IT"

"ETHEL.. CALL YOUR SISTER! THEY'RE GIVING A FREE SPRAY HOSE WITH EACH 5-GALLON PURCHASE!"

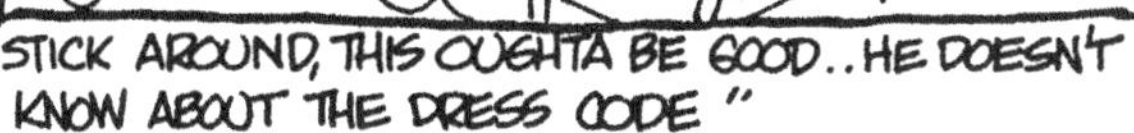

"STICK AROUND, THIS OUGHTA BE GOOD.. HE DOESN'T KNOW ABOUT THE DRESS CODE"

"IT'S HIM AGAIN, ISN'T IT?!"

"...OKAY.. SO THERE I WAS SITTING ALL ALONE, **AS USUAL**, I MIGHT ADD... WHEN SUDDENLY..."

"WELL THEN, HERE'S TO ME"

"IRONIC...THE LAST THING HE SAID WAS 'I DON'T FEEL SAFE'"

"THIS MAN NEXT TO ME SAYS HE WANTS TO KILL YOU THE NEXT TIME YOU SAY 'GOODBYE MISTER CHIPS'"

"IF IT WASN'T FOR THAT BARKING ELEPHANT THIS WOULD BE A TOTAL RIPOFF"

"LIONEL WRITES SONGS FROM HIS PERSONAL EXPERIENCES....
MOSTLY MARCHING TUNES ABOUT HIM AND HIS FRIENDS"



"KEEP YOUR EYES OPEN...YOU NEVER KNOW WHEN YOU'RE GONNA
RUN ACROSS ONE OF THEM CLOWNS WITH THEIR TOPS DOWN!"

"MORT.. YOU'D BETTER TAKE THIS SITTING DOWN... THEY'VE ALREADY GOT ONE "

"IF IT'S SUPPOSED TO BE SO GOOD, WHY HASN'T HE MOVED YET ? "

"A COLA FOR THE KID AND TWO CAFFEINES FOR US"

"THEY TOOK OUT THE TIME CLOCKS AND PUT US ON THE HONOR SYSTEM.. NOW WE CAN ALL BEAT THAT RUSH-HOUR TRAFFIC"

WORLDS LARGEST
TOOTHPICK CASTLE

$11.95 for a full year of all four comics or just one - same price.  Email us at mrboffo@mrboffo.com, sign up online at www.mrboffo.com or www.catswithhands.com, or write Neatly Chiseled Features, N1870 Loramoor Drive, Lake Geneva, WI.53147, 262-248-9460 phone  262-248-3431 fax

- • WILLY 'N ETHEL

- • MISTER BOFFO

- • CATS WITH HANDS

Visit us at www.mrboffo.com for books, originals, animations, comic videos, paintings, novelty albums, and a 30,000 joke archive

- •




Neatly Chiseled Features
N1870 Loramoor Drive
Lake Geneva, WI.  53147
262-248-9460
www.mrboffo.com
email:  mrboffo@mrboffo.com
ISBN13: 9780943084299

Printed in the United States
31112LVS00001B/177-200

9 780943 084299

Made in the USA
Monee, IL
09 May 2026